Oprah's
THE LIFE
YOU WANT

BOOK LOVER'S
JOURNAL

> " A great book not only enhances your life experience, but it can also change you.

—OPRAH

Oprah's
THE LIFE
YOU WANT

BOOK LOVER'S
JOURNAL

READING IS MY ABSOLUTE favorite way to spend time. Reading opens a person up. It exposes you and gives you access to anything your mind can hold. When I learned to read at age 3, I discovered there was a whole world to conquer that went beyond our farm in Mississippi.

Back then, books were a way to escape, but I've since learned they offer so much more. They are novels that cut us to our core, memoirs that show us what people are truly capable of, spiritual guides that connect us to the divine, poetry collections that tackle life's eternal questions, histories that make sense of our shared past, roadmaps that take us on a journey to authenticity, and, above all, stories that leave us forever transformed.

Now, you know that I love to share the books that have hooked me, starting way back with *The Deep End of the Ocean*, by Jacquelyn Mitchard, the first Oprah's Book Club selection. We've put this journal together to give you a place to capture the books that you've loved, as well as the sentences that stopped you in your tracks and the titles you want to read next. It has prompts to help you remember old favorites and new recommendations—novels, memoirs, nonfiction, poetry, short story collections, book club picks— and plenty of space for notes.

As you fill out the pages, I hope this will become a collection of the books you didn't know you needed, the authors you've loved, and the lessons you've learned about the world and your place in it. Let's read on.

Oprah

For book reviews and to learn of Oprah's next Book Club selections, visit **OprahDaily.com**, and follow us 📷 **@Oprahsbookclub**

Table of Contents

Books are knowledge. Books are reflection. Books change your mind.

—TONI MORRISON

66

I am so impressed again with the life-giving power of literature.

—MAYA ANGELOU

Books That Made a Difference

The prompts in this section are focused on helping you recall the books that moved you, changed you, inspired you. You don't need to fill out all these pages right away. Maybe you haven't come across a memorable memoir or a love story for the ages... yet. You can return to these pages throughout your reading journey.

MY FAVORITE BOOK OF ALL TIME

Title: _____

_____

Why I loved it:

_____

_____

_____

_____

_____

_____

_____

_____

The time in my life when I read it:

_____

_____

_____

_____

_____

_____

"I've talked a lot about how much *Beloved* meant to me. I believe Toni Morrison was our conscience. Our seer. Our truth-teller. She was a magician with language, who understood the Power of words. She used them to roil us, to wake us, to educate us, and help us grapple with our deepest wounds. Nowhere more than in *Beloved*."

—OPRAH

The quotes I always remember:

_____

_____

_____

_____

_____

_____

_____

_____

_____

_____

_____

_____

_____

_____

_____

_____

THE FIRST BOOK THAT
MADE ME FEEL SEEN

Title: _____

_____

What resonated most with me:

_____

_____

_____

_____

_____

_____

_____

The scene I continue to think about:

_____

_____

_____

_____

_____

_____

_____

"Maya Angelou's autobiography *I Know Why the Caged Bird Sings*
was the first book I ever read that made me feel my life as
a 'colored girl' growing up in Mississippi deserved validation.
I loved it from the opening line."

—OPRAH

Quotes that hit home:

_____

_____

_____

_____

_____

_____

_____

_____

The truest part of the book:

_____

_____

_____

_____

_____

_____

THE *OLD* CLASSIC I LOVE

Title: _____

_____

Why it struck a chord:

_____

_____

_____

_____

_____

_____

_____

_____

The character I'll always remember and why:

_____

_____

_____

_____

_____

_____

"The Grapes of Wrath is one of my favorite books. I found it an eye opening experience traveling with the Joads, enduring their hunger and hardships. Nelson Mandela once told me that of the many books read in prison that was one of the most important: 'When I closed that book, I was a different man. It enriched my powers of thinking and discipline, and my relationships.' And I've never forgotten that."

—OPRAH

The quotes I'll always remember:

_____

_____

_____

_____

_____

_____

_____

_____

A lesson I'll take from this book:

_____

_____

_____

_____

_____

_____

_____

THE *NEW* CLASSIC I LOVE

Title: _____

_____

Why it struck a chord:

_____

_____

_____

_____

_____

_____

_____

The character I'll always remember and why:

_____

_____

_____

_____

_____

_____

"*The Story of Edgar Sawtelle*, by David Wroblewski, is so engaging, so gripping, so epic that I wanted absolutely everybody to share the joy of this novel. I think that it's right up there with the greatest American novels ever written, up there with Steinbeck and even Harper Lee."
—OPRAH

The quotes I'll always remember:

_____

_____

_____

_____

_____

_____

A lesson I'll take from this book:

_____

_____

_____

_____

_____

_____

_____

THE NOVEL THAT HIT ME HARD

Title: _____

_____

Why it struck a chord:

_____

_____

_____

_____

_____

_____

_____

The moment that was most powerful:

_____

_____

_____

_____

_____

_____

_____

"The Water Dancer, by Ta-Nehisi Coates, is an incredible book—
as beautiful as it is tragic.... I knew early on the book was going to
cut me up. I ended up with my soul pierced."
—OPRAH

Quote I'll always remember:

_____

_____

_____

_____

_____

_____

_____

_____

_____

_____

_____

_____

_____

_____

_____

_____

_____

_____

_____

THE SELF-HELP BOOK THAT WAS A REVELATION

Title: _____

_____

What surprised me most about this book:

_____

_____

_____

_____

_____

_____

_____

_____

How it helped me live differently:

_____

_____

_____

_____

_____

_____

"I'd never recommended a book in the spiritual or self-help genre before, but because *A New Earth*, by Eckhart Tolle, had such a profound impact on me, I thought others might also be struck by the idea of putting the ego in check and becoming more aware of being rather than doing."
—OPRAH

The advice I'll take with me:

_____

_____

_____

_____

_____

_____

_____

_____

_____

_____

_____

_____

_____

_____

_____

_____

_____

A LOVE STORY FOR THE AGES

Title: _____

_____

Why this love story above all others:

_____

_____

_____

_____

_____

_____

_____

_____

_____

_____

_____

_____

_____

_____

_____

_____

_____

_____

"Zora Neale Hurston's classic *Their Eyes Were Watching God* is my favorite love story of all time. Janie Mae Crawford spends almost two decades with abusive, domineering men but eventually finds true love with Tea Cake. In the time they have together, he teaches her to open her heart to the world."

—OPRAH

Quote that I'll never forget:

_____

_____

_____

_____

_____

_____

_____

_____

_____

_____

_____

_____

_____

_____

_____

_____

THE BOOK I GO BACK TO

Title: _____

_____

Why I return to it:

_____

_____

_____

_____

_____

_____

_____

_____

_____

_____

_____

_____

_____

_____

_____

_____

_____

> "I rarely read novels again. But I read *The Bluest Eye* every few years and still feel altered every time by the character Pecola Breedlove and Toni Morrison's adept portrayal of life in this community."
>
> —OPRAH

What I got from it the first time I read it:

_____

_____

_____

_____

_____

_____

What I got from it this time:

_____

_____

_____

_____

_____

_____

_____

_____

66

Reading for the pure pleasure of it, for the beautiful stillness that surrounds you when you hear an author's words reverberating in your head.

—PAUL AUSTER

A MEMORABLE MEMOIR

Title: _____

_____

Why I loved their story:

_____

_____

_____

_____

_____

_____

_____

_____

The quote I loved:

_____

_____

_____

_____

_____

_____

"There are so many lessons to be learned from *Finding Me*, a breathtaking memoir about triumphing over adversity and trauma. Viola Davis leaves it all on the page—from her beginnings in South Carolina as the fifth of six children born in a sharecropper's shack to acclaim as an actor, producer, and philanthropist. I was so moved by this book that I just had to share it with the entire Oprah's Book Club audience."

—OPRAH

The most profound life truth:

_____

_____

_____

_____

_____

_____

_____

_____

_____

_____

_____

_____

_____

_____

_____

_____

_____

_____

A COMING OF AGE...THAT KEEPS COMING BACK TO MIND

Title: _____

_____

When I read it:

_____

_____

_____

_____

The reason I love it:

_____

_____

_____

_____

_____

_____

_____

_____

_____

"Page after page of reading *White Oleander*, by Janet Fitch, I fell in love with a story that deeply moved me and vivid passages that described the sky as the color of peaches and compared sorrow to the taste of a copper penny."

—OPRAH

The quote that took my breath away:

_____

_____

_____

_____

_____

_____

What was different about this story of transformation:

_____

_____

_____

_____

_____

_____

_____

_____

THE BOOK THAT LIGHTENS ANY DAY

Title: _____

_____

The reason it's just so good:

_____

_____

_____

_____

_____

_____

_____

_____

_____

The quote that never fails to make me laugh:

_____

_____

_____

_____

_____

"I start my mornings with a poem, and I end my evenings with a poem. Right now, my favorite book of poetry is Mark Nepo's *The Half-Life of Angels.*"
—OPRAH

The scene I go back to:

_____

_____

_____

_____

_____

_____

_____

_____

_____

_____

The friend I could send who needs a lift:

_____

_____

_____

_____

_____

_____

THE BOOK THAT INTRODUCED ME TO ANOTHER WORLD

Title: _____

_____

Where it was set:

_____

_____

_____

_____

_____

What I loved most about that world:

_____

_____

_____

_____

_____

_____

_____

_____

"The Covenant of Water, by Abraham Verghese, is epic. It's transportive. It's gorgeous writing in generations of stories. Many moments, I had to stop and remember to breathe. Months later the extravagant humanity coursing through the narrative still abides with me."
—OPRAH

What it showed me that I hadn't seen before:

_____
_____
_____
_____
_____
_____
_____
_____

How it affected how I see my part of the world:

_____
_____
_____
_____
_____
_____
_____
_____

FAVORITE COOKBOOK

Title: _____

_____

Why I loved it:

_____

_____

_____

_____

_____

_____

_____

_____

_____

_____

_____

_____

_____

_____

_____

_____

_____

> "Anybody can make anything in Jamie Oliver's *5 Ingredients: Quick and Easy Food*. Anybody! I feel chef-like when I cook from it."
> —OPRAH

My favorite recipes:

_____

_____

_____

_____

_____

_____

_____

_____

_____

Notes:

_____

_____

_____

_____

_____

_____

_____

_____

THE COFFEE TABLE BOOK TO LONG FOR

Title: _____

_____

What it's about:

_____

_____

_____

_____

_____

_____

Best inspiration from it:

_____

_____

_____

_____

_____

_____

_____

_____

"I so enjoy thumbing through the pages of *The Way We Live*, by Stafford Cliff—it's like being on a train, passing other people's houses, and getting to see a small minute of how they live."

—OPRAH

Why it's so beautiful to me:

_____

_____

_____

_____

_____

_____

_____

_____

_____

_____

Who might I give this to:

_____

_____

_____

_____

_____

_____

_____

A BOOK THAT CHANGED
MY MIND

Title: _____

_____

What it's about:

_____

_____

_____

_____

_____

_____

_____

What I used to think:

_____

_____

_____

_____

_____

_____

_____

"*Discover the Power Within You*, by Eric Butterworth, changed my perspective on life and religion. Butterworth teaches that God isn't 'up there.' He exists inside each one of us, and it's up to us to seek the divine within. As he writes, 'the greatest mistake is in believing that we are "only human"…. We are human in expression but divine in creation and limitless in potentiality.'"
—OPRAH

What I think now:

_____

_____

_____

_____

_____

_____

_____

The thing that shifted my opinion:

_____

_____

_____

_____

_____

_____

_____

_____

THE MOST IMPORTANT BOOK ANYONE SHOULD READ

Title: _____

_____

What it's about:

_____

_____

_____

_____

_____

_____

Why it's so compelling:

_____

_____

_____

_____

_____

_____

_____

_____

"Caste, by Isabel Wilkerson, is an essential read for anyone who cares to really understand the current state of America. It explains where we are, in terms of inequality and racial injustice. I sent this book to 500 people in leadership positions—from senators and mayors to heads of universities—hoping if everyone read it and spread the word, we might save ourselves."
—OPRAH

Who should read a copy of it now, and why:

_____

_____

_____

_____

Quote I loved:

_____

_____

_____

_____

_____

_____

_____

_____

_____

> ## "Reading is a conversation."
>
> —ALBERTO MANGUEL

Gathering Together

You may be part of a book club now or gearing up to start one with friends and neighbors—either way, these pages are meant to help you make the most of your time and keep track of your thoughts on each meeting.

BOOK CLUB MEMBERS

NAME

DATES JOINED/LEFT GROUP

_____   _____

_____   _____

_____   _____

_____   _____

_____   _____

_____   _____

_____   _____

_____   _____

_____   _____

ADVICE FOR LAUNCHING YOUR OWN

Some book clubs start out strong and then dwindle away. Here's how yours can stay the course.

Never choose a book unless one person has read it.

This is helpful for a few reasons: One, it means that you have someone who can lead the discussion that month. For another, it means at least one member thinks your group will have enough to talk about. What it doesn't mean is that everyone will like the book—but that's okay. A robust conversation can clarify what each of you did (or did not) find important/ meaningful/ transcendent. The back-and-forth might even change your mind.

Change up your book selections.

If you pick a long novel, like *The Covenant of Water* or *The Pillars of the Earth*, you might want to pick a shorter read for your next meeting so that people don't feel overwhelmed. If your book club has been going a few years, you might mix genres to keep conversations fresh—choosing a memoir, a collection of poetry, a self-help book—or pick a book that's just been translated or one that's recently re-released.

Don't freak out about the food.

As writer and longtime book club host Liesl Schillinger says, "It's Book Club, not Gourmet Club." A home-cooked meal inspired by the setting of this month's choice sounds terrific, but you know what's also delicious? Carry out.

Respect the calendar.

To keep momentum, you'll want to meet every 6 to 8 weeks, but you'll likely want to wrap up your book club year in early November, because no matter how many good intentions, no one will be able to meet amid the annual steeple chase that is Thanksgiving to New Year's.

Consider asking the author to drop in.

Jean Hanff Korelitz, author of *The Plot*, started a company, BooktheWriter. com, to connect book clubs with book writers. She says many writers are happy to Zoom into a night's conversation or stop by if it's local. It's polite to offer payment and cover expenses if it's in person and, of course, show support by purchasing the book. Inviting the author is a unique way to celebrate your first, tenth, or even 20th book club anniversary.

BOOKS WE'VE READ

1

Title: _____

When and where we discussed the book: _____

Food served: _____

The kind of book (novel, memoir, poetry, graphic novel, etc.): _____
_____

The plot in one sentence: _____
_____

What most of us liked:

_____
_____
_____
_____
_____

What one of us didn't like:

_____
_____
_____
_____

Our favorite quote in the book:

_____

_____

_____

_____

_____

_____

My favorite quote from our conversation:

_____

_____

_____

_____

_____

Notes:

_____

_____

_____

_____

_____

BOOKS WE'VE READ

2

Title: _____

When and where we discussed the book: _____

Food served: _____

The kind of book (novel, memoir, poetry, graphic novel, etc.): _____

_____

The plot in one sentence: _____

_____

What most of us liked:

_____

_____

_____

_____

_____

What one of us didn't like:

_____

_____

_____

_____

Our favorite quote in the book:

_____

_____

_____

_____

_____

_____

My favorite quote from our conversation:

_____

_____

_____

_____

_____

_____

Notes:

_____

_____

_____

_____

_____

_____

BOOKS WE'VE READ

3

Title: _____

When and where we discussed the book: _____

Food served: _____

The kind of book (novel, memoir, poetry, graphic novel, etc.): _____

_____

The plot in one sentence: _____

_____

What most of us liked:

_____

_____

_____

_____

_____

What one of us didn't like:

_____

_____

_____

_____

Our favorite quote in the book:

_____

_____

_____

_____

_____

_____

My favorite quote from our conversation:

_____

_____

_____

_____

_____

_____

Notes:

_____

_____

_____

_____

_____

_____

BOOKS WE'VE READ

4

Title: _____

When and where we discussed the book: _____

Food served: _____

The kind of book (novel, memoir, poetry, graphic novel, etc.): _____
_____

The plot in one sentence: _____
_____

What most of us liked:

_____
_____
_____
_____
_____

What one of us didn't like:

_____
_____
_____
_____

Our favorite quote in the book:

_____

_____

_____

_____

_____

_____

My favorite quote from our conversation:

_____

_____

_____

_____

_____

_____

Notes:

_____

_____

_____

_____

_____

_____

_____

BOOKS WE'VE READ

5

Title: _____

When and where we discussed the book: _____

Food served: _____

The kind of book (novel, memoir, poetry, graphic novel, etc.): _____
_____

The plot in one sentence: _____
_____

What most of us liked:
_____
_____
_____
_____
_____

What one of us didn't like:
_____
_____
_____
_____

Our favorite quote in the book:

_____

_____

_____

_____

_____

_____

My favorite quote from our conversation:

_____

_____

_____

_____

_____

_____

Notes:

_____

_____

_____

_____

_____

_____

BOOKS WE'VE READ

6

Title: _____

When and where we discussed the book: _____

Food served: _____

The kind of book (novel, memoir, poetry, graphic novel, etc.): _____
_____

The plot in one sentence: _____
_____

What most of us liked:
_____
_____
_____
_____
_____

What one of us didn't like:
_____
_____
_____
_____

Our favorite quote in the book:

_____

_____

_____

_____

_____

_____

My favorite quote from our conversation:

_____

_____

_____

_____

_____

_____

Notes:

_____

_____

_____

_____

_____

_____

BOOKS WE'VE READ

7

Title: _____

When and where we discussed the book: _____

Food served: _____

The kind of book (novel, memoir, poetry, graphic novel, etc.): _____
_____

The plot in one sentence: _____
_____

What most of us liked:

_____
_____
_____
_____
_____

What one of us didn't like:

_____
_____
_____
_____

Our favorite quote in the book:

_____

_____

_____

_____

_____

_____

My favorite quote from our conversation:

_____

_____

_____

_____

_____

_____

Notes:

_____

_____

_____

_____

_____

_____

BOOKS WE'VE READ

8

Title: _____

When and where we discussed the book: _____

Food served: _____

The kind of book (novel, memoir, poetry, graphic novel, etc.): _____
_____

The plot in one sentence: _____
_____

What most of us liked:

_____

_____

_____

_____

_____

What one of us didn't like:

_____

_____

_____

_____

Our favorite quote in the book:

_____

_____

_____

_____

_____

_____

My favorite quote from our conversation:

_____

_____

_____

_____

_____

Notes:

_____

_____

_____

_____

_____

BOOKS WE'VE READ

9

Title: _____

When and where we discussed the book: _____

Food served: _____

The kind of book (novel, memoir, poetry, graphic novel, etc.): _____
_____

The plot in one sentence: _____
_____

What most of us liked:
_____
_____
_____
_____
_____

What one of us didn't like:
_____
_____
_____
_____

Our favorite quote in the book:

_____

_____

_____

_____

_____

_____

My favorite quote from our conversation:

_____

_____

_____

_____

_____

_____

Notes:

_____

_____

_____

_____

_____

_____

BOOKS WE'VE READ

Title: _____

When and where we discussed the book: _____

Food served: _____

The kind of book (novel, memoir, poetry, graphic novel, etc.): _____

_____

The plot in one sentence: _____

_____

What most of us liked:

_____

_____

_____

_____

_____

What one of us didn't like:

_____

_____

_____

_____

Our favorite quote in the book:

_____

_____

_____

_____

_____

_____

My favorite quote from our conversation:

_____

_____

_____

_____

_____

Notes:

_____

_____

_____

_____

_____

BOOKS WE'VE READ

Title: _____

When and where we discussed the book: _____

Food served: _____

The kind of book (novel, memoir, poetry, graphic novel, etc.): _____

_____

The plot in one sentence: _____

_____

What most of us liked:

_____

_____

_____

_____

_____

What one of us didn't like:

_____

_____

_____

_____

Our favorite quote in the book:

_____

_____

_____

_____

_____

_____

My favorite quote from our conversation:

_____

_____

_____

_____

_____

Notes:

_____

_____

_____

_____

_____

_____

BOOKS WE'VE READ

12

Title: _____

When and where we discussed the book: _____

Food served: _____

The kind of book (novel, memoir, poetry, graphic novel, etc.): _____

_____

The plot in one sentence: _____

_____

What most of us liked:

_____

_____

_____

_____

_____

What one of us didn't like:

_____

_____

_____

_____

Our favorite quote in the book:

_____

_____

_____

_____

_____

_____

My favorite quote from our conversation:

_____

_____

_____

_____

_____

Notes:

_____

_____

_____

_____

_____

_____

66

When I read, I like to go somewhere else in my mind with stories that touch our real world without taking place in it.

—TOMI ADEYEMI

BOOKS WE'VE READ

13

Title: _____

When and where we discussed the book: _____

Food served: _____

The kind of book (novel, memoir, poetry, graphic novel, etc.): _____
_____

The plot in one sentence: _____
_____

What most of us liked:

_____
_____
_____
_____
_____

What one of us didn't like:

_____
_____
_____
_____

Our favorite quote in the book:

_____

_____

_____

_____

_____

_____

My favorite quote from our conversation:

_____

_____

_____

_____

_____

Notes:

_____

_____

_____

_____

_____

_____

BOOKS WE'VE READ

14

Title: _____

When and where we discussed the book: _____

Food served: _____

The kind of book (novel, memoir, poetry, graphic novel, etc.): _____

_____

The plot in one sentence: _____

_____

What most of us liked:

_____

_____

_____

_____

_____

What one of us didn't like:

_____

_____

_____

_____

Our favorite quote in the book:

_____

_____

_____

_____

_____

_____

My favorite quote from our conversation:

_____

_____

_____

_____

_____

_____

Notes:

_____

_____

_____

_____

_____

_____

BOOKS WE'VE READ

15

Title: _____

When and where we discussed the book: _____

Food served: _____

The kind of book (novel, memoir, poetry, graphic novel, etc.): _____

_____

The plot in one sentence: _____

_____

What most of us liked:

_____

_____

_____

_____

_____

What one of us didn't like:

_____

_____

_____

_____

Our favorite quote in the book:

_____

_____

_____

_____

_____

_____

My favorite quote from our conversation:

_____

_____

_____

_____

_____

_____

Notes:

_____

_____

_____

_____

_____

_____

BOOKS WE'VE READ

Title: _____

When and where we discussed the book: _____

Food served: _____

The kind of book (novel, memoir, poetry, graphic novel, etc.): _____

_____

The plot in one sentence: _____

_____

What most of us liked:

_____

_____

_____

_____

_____

What one of us didn't like:

_____

_____

_____

_____

Our favorite quote in the book:

_____

_____

_____

_____

_____

_____

My favorite quote from our conversation:

_____

_____

_____

_____

_____

_____

Notes:

_____

_____

_____

_____

_____

_____

BOOKS WE'VE READ

17

Title: _____

When and where we discussed the book: _____

Food served: _____

The kind of book (novel, memoir, poetry, graphic novel, etc.): _____
_____

The plot in one sentence: _____
_____

What most of us liked:

_____
_____
_____
_____
_____

What one of us didn't like:

_____
_____
_____
_____

Our favorite quote in the book:

_____

_____

_____

_____

_____

_____

My favorite quote from our conversation:

_____

_____

_____

_____

_____

_____

Notes:

_____

_____

_____

_____

_____

_____

BOOKS WE'VE READ

18

Title: _____

When and where we discussed the book: _____

Food served: _____

The kind of book (novel, memoir, poetry, graphic novel, etc.): _____
_____

The plot in one sentence: _____
_____

What most of us liked:
_____
_____
_____
_____
_____

What one of us didn't like:
_____
_____
_____
_____

Our favorite quote in the book:

_____

_____

_____

_____

_____

_____

My favorite quote from our conversation:

_____

_____

_____

_____

_____

_____

Notes:

_____

_____

_____

_____

_____

_____

BOOKS WE'VE READ

19

Title: _____

When and where we discussed the book: _____

Food served: _____

The kind of book (novel, memoir, poetry, graphic novel, etc.): _____
_____

The plot in one sentence: _____
_____

What most of us liked:

_____

_____

_____

_____

_____

What one of us didn't like:

_____

_____

_____

_____

Our favorite quote in the book:

_____

_____

_____

_____

_____

_____

My favorite quote from our conversation:

_____

_____

_____

_____

_____

Notes:

_____

_____

_____

_____

_____

_____

BOOKS WE'VE READ

20

Title: _____

When and where we discussed the book: _____

Food served: _____

The kind of book (novel, memoir, poetry, graphic novel, etc.): _____

_____

The plot in one sentence: _____

_____

What most of us liked:

_____

_____

_____

_____

_____

What one of us didn't like:

_____

_____

_____

_____

Our favorite quote in the book:

_____

_____

_____

_____

_____

_____

My favorite quote from our conversation:

_____

_____

_____

_____

_____

_____

Notes:

_____

_____

_____

_____

_____

_____

_____

BOOKS WE'VE READ

21

Title: _____

When and where we discussed the book: _____

Food served: _____

The kind of book (novel, memoir, poetry, graphic novel, etc.): _____

The plot in one sentence: _____

What most of us liked:

_____
_____
_____
_____
_____

What one of us didn't like:

_____
_____
_____
_____

Our favorite quote in the book:

_____

_____

_____

_____

_____

_____

My favorite quote from our conversation:

_____

_____

_____

_____

_____

Notes:

_____

_____

_____

_____

_____

_____

BOOKS WE'VE READ

22

Title: _____

When and where we discussed the book: _____

Food served: _____

The kind of book (novel, memoir, poetry, graphic novel, etc.): _____
_____

The plot in one sentence: _____
_____

What most of us liked:

_____
_____
_____
_____
_____

What one of us didn't like:

_____
_____
_____
_____

Our favorite quote in the book:

_____

_____

_____

_____

_____

_____

My favorite quote from our conversation:

_____

_____

_____

_____

_____

_____

Notes:

_____

_____

_____

_____

_____

BOOKS WE'VE READ

23

Title: _____

When and where we discussed the book: _____

Food served: _____

The kind of book (novel, memoir, poetry, graphic novel, etc.): _____
_____

The plot in one sentence: _____
_____

What most of us liked:

_____
_____
_____
_____
_____

What one of us didn't like:

_____
_____
_____
_____

Our favorite quote in the book:

_____

_____

_____

_____

_____

_____

My favorite quote from our conversation:

_____

_____

_____

_____

_____

Notes:

_____

_____

_____

_____

_____

_____

BOOKS WE'VE READ

Title: _____

When and where we discussed the book: _____

Food served: _____

The kind of book (novel, memoir, poetry, graphic novel, etc.): _____

_____

The plot in one sentence: _____

_____

What most of us liked:

_____

_____

_____

_____

_____

What one of us didn't like:

_____

_____

_____

_____

Our favorite quote in the book:

_____

_____

_____

_____

_____

_____

My favorite quote from our conversation:

_____

_____

_____

_____

_____

_____

Notes:

_____

_____

_____

_____

_____

_____

BOOKS WE MIGHT READ

Almost every book club has been there: Having just finished the current selection, somebody asks, "So what are we going to read next?" To avoid the inevitable whirlpool of proposals and counterproposals (Longer! Shorter! Funnier! Sadder!), start a list of titles that sound like good reads—and also offer a lot to discuss.

TITLE	AUTHOR

PAGE COUNT	GENRE	WHY
_____	_____	_____
_____	_____	_____
_____	_____	_____
_____	_____	_____
_____	_____	_____
_____	_____	_____
_____	_____	_____
_____	_____	_____
_____	_____	_____
_____	_____	_____

BOOKS WE MIGHT READ

<u>TITLE</u>   <u>AUTHOR</u>

_____   _____

_____   _____

_____   _____

_____   _____

_____   _____

_____   _____

_____   _____

_____   _____

_____   _____

_____   _____

PAGE COUNT	GENRE	WHY

BOOKS WE MIGHT READ

	TITLE	AUTHOR

PAGE COUNT	GENRE	WHY

BOOKS WE MIGHT READ

TITLE	AUTHOR

PAGE COUNT	GENRE	WHY

"

I'm alone, with what
the book and I have to
offer each other.

—MARGO JEFFERSON

Reading Alone

As you continue your reading journey, keep track of the books you've read and what you thought about the stories, the writing and the effects they had on you.

BOOKS I'VE FINISHED

Use these pages to capture your thoughts on the novels, memoirs, nonfiction, poetry, short story collections, book club picks—in short, *all* the books—that were too good to put down.

Title: _____

When and where I read the book: _____

The kind of book (novel, memoir, poetry, graphic novel, etc.): _____
_____

The plot in one sentence: _____
_____

What I liked best about the book:
_____
_____
_____
_____
_____

A reason the book resonated at this moment in my life:
_____
_____
_____
_____
_____

How I see the world (or myself) differently having read this book?

_____

_____

_____

_____

_____

Quotes I loved from the book:

_____

_____

_____

_____

_____

_____

_____

_____

_____

_____

_____

_____

_____

_____

_____

BOOKS I'VE FINISHED

Title: _____

When and where I read the book: _____

The kind of book (novel, memoir, poetry, graphic novel, etc.): _____

_____

The plot in one sentence: _____

_____

What I liked best about the book:

_____

_____

_____

_____

_____

A reason the book resonated at this moment in my life:

_____

_____

_____

_____

_____

How I see the world (or myself) differently having read this book?

_____

_____

_____

_____

_____

Quotes I loved from the book:

_____

_____

_____

_____

_____

_____

_____

_____

_____

_____

_____

_____

_____

_____

BOOKS I'VE FINISHED

Title: _____

When and where I read the book: _____

The kind of book (novel, memoir, poetry, graphic novel, etc.): _____
_____

The plot in one sentence: _____
_____

What I liked best about the book:
_____
_____
_____
_____
_____

A reason the book resonated at this moment in my life:
_____
_____
_____
_____
_____

How I see the world (or myself) differently having read this book?

_____

_____

_____

_____

_____

Quotes I loved from the book:

_____

_____

_____

_____

_____

_____

_____

_____

_____

_____

_____

_____

_____

_____

_____

BOOKS I'VE FINISHED

Title: _____

When and where I read the book: _____

The kind of book (novel, memoir, poetry, graphic novel, etc.): _____
_____

The plot in one sentence: _____
_____

What I liked best about the book:
_____
_____
_____
_____
_____

A reason the book resonated at this moment in my life:
_____
_____
_____
_____
_____

How I see the world (or myself) differently having read this book?

_____

_____

_____

_____

_____

Quotes I loved from the book:

_____

_____

_____

_____

_____

_____

_____

_____

_____

_____

_____

_____

_____

_____

_____

BOOKS I'VE FINISHED

Title: _____

When and where I read the book: _____

The kind of book (novel, memoir, poetry, graphic novel, etc.): _____

_____

The plot in one sentence: _____

_____

What I liked best about the book:

_____

_____

_____

_____

_____

A reason the book resonated at this moment in my life:

_____

_____

_____

_____

_____

How I see the world (or myself) differently having read this book?

_____

_____

_____

_____

_____

Quotes I loved from the book:

_____

_____

_____

_____

_____

_____

_____

_____

_____

_____

_____

_____

_____

_____

_____

BOOKS I'VE FINISHED

Title: _____

When and where I read the book: _____

The kind of book (novel, memoir, poetry, graphic novel, etc.): _____

_____

The plot in one sentence: _____

_____

What I liked best about the book:

_____

_____

_____

_____

_____

A reason the book resonated at this moment in my life:

_____

_____

_____

_____

_____

How I see the world (or myself) differently having read this book?

_____

_____

_____

_____

_____

Quotes I loved from the book:

_____

_____

_____

_____

_____

_____

_____

_____

_____

_____

_____

_____

_____

_____

_____

BOOKS I'VE FINISHED

Title: _____

When and where I read the book: _____

The kind of book (novel, memoir, poetry, graphic novel, etc.): _____
_____

The plot in one sentence: _____
_____

What I liked best about the book:
_____
_____
_____
_____
_____

A reason the book resonated at this moment in my life:
_____
_____
_____
_____
_____

How I see the world (or myself) differently having read this book?

_____

_____

_____

_____

_____

Quotes I loved from the book:

_____

_____

_____

_____

_____

_____

_____

_____

_____

_____

_____

_____

_____

_____

BOOKS I'VE FINISHED

Title: _____

When and where I read the book: _____

The kind of book (novel, memoir, poetry, graphic novel, etc.): _____
_____

The plot in one sentence: _____
_____

What I liked best about the book:
_____
_____
_____
_____
_____

A reason the book resonated at this moment in my life:
_____
_____
_____
_____
_____

How I see the world (or myself) differently having read this book?

_____

_____

_____

_____

_____

Quotes I loved from the book:

_____

_____

_____

_____

_____

_____

_____

_____

_____

_____

_____

_____

_____

BOOKS I'VE FINISHED

Title: _____

When and where I read the book: _____

The kind of book (novel, memoir, poetry, graphic novel, etc.): _____

_____

The plot in one sentence: _____

_____

What I liked best about the book:

_____

_____

_____

_____

_____

A reason the book resonated at this moment in my life:

_____

_____

_____

_____

_____

How I see the world (or myself) differently having read this book?

_____

_____

_____

_____

_____

Quotes I loved from the book:

_____

_____

_____

_____

_____

_____

_____

_____

_____

_____

_____

_____

_____

_____

_____

BOOKS I'VE FINISHED

Title: _____

When and where I read the book: _____

The kind of book (novel, memoir, poetry, graphic novel, etc.): _____
_____

The plot in one sentence: _____
_____

What I liked best about the book:

_____
_____
_____
_____
_____

A reason the book resonated at this moment in my life:

_____
_____
_____
_____
_____

How I see the world (or myself) differently having read this book?

_____

_____

_____

_____

_____

Quotes I loved from the book:

_____

_____

_____

_____

_____

_____

_____

_____

_____

_____

_____

_____

_____

_____

BOOKS I'VE FINISHED

Title: _____

When and where I read the book: _____

The kind of book (novel, memoir, poetry, graphic novel, etc.): _____

_____

The plot in one sentence: _____

_____

What I liked best about the book:

_____

_____

_____

_____

_____

A reason the book resonated at this moment in my life:

_____

_____

_____

_____

_____

How I see the world (or myself) differently having read this book?

_____

_____

_____

_____

_____

Quotes I loved from the book:

_____

_____

_____

_____

_____

_____

_____

_____

_____

_____

_____

_____

_____

BOOKS I'VE FINISHED

Title: _____

When and where I read the book: _____

The kind of book (novel, memoir, poetry, graphic novel, etc.): _____
_____

The plot in one sentence: _____
_____

What I liked best about the book:

_____
_____
_____
_____
_____

A reason the book resonated at this moment in my life:

_____
_____
_____
_____
_____

How I see the world (or myself) differently having read this book?

_____

_____

_____

_____

_____

Quotes I loved from the book:

_____

_____

_____

_____

_____

_____

_____

_____

_____

_____

_____

_____

_____

**We read books to
find out who we are.**

—URSULA K. LE GUIN

BOOKS I'VE FINISHED

Title: _____

When and where I read the book: _____

The kind of book (novel, memoir, poetry, graphic novel, etc.): _____

_____

The plot in one sentence: _____

_____

What I liked best about the book:

_____

_____

_____

_____

_____

A reason the book resonated at this moment in my life:

_____

_____

_____

_____

_____

How I see the world (or myself) differently having read this book?

_____

_____

_____

_____

_____

Quotes I loved from the book:

_____

_____

_____

_____

_____

_____

_____

_____

_____

_____

_____

_____

_____

_____

BOOKS I'VE FINISHED

Title: _____

When and where I read the book: _____

The kind of book (novel, memoir, poetry, graphic novel, etc.): _____

_____

The plot in one sentence: _____

_____

What I liked best about the book:

_____

_____

_____

_____

_____

A reason the book resonated at this moment in my life:

_____

_____

_____

_____

_____

How I see the world (or myself) differently having read this book?

_____

_____

_____

_____

_____

Quotes I loved from the book:

_____

_____

_____

_____

_____

_____

_____

_____

_____

_____

_____

_____

_____

_____

BOOKS I'VE FINISHED

Title: _____

When and where I read the book: _____

The kind of book (novel, memoir, poetry, graphic novel, etc.): _____

_____

The plot in one sentence: _____

_____

What I liked best about the book:

_____

_____

_____

_____

_____

A reason the book resonated at this moment in my life:

_____

_____

_____

_____

_____

How I see the world (or myself) differently having read this book?

_____

_____

_____

_____

_____

Quotes I loved from the book:

_____

_____

_____

_____

_____

_____

_____

_____

_____

_____

_____

_____

_____

_____

_____

_____

BOOKS I'VE FINISHED

Title: _____

When and where I read the book: _____

The kind of book (novel, memoir, poetry, graphic novel, etc.): _____

_____

The plot in one sentence: _____

_____

What I liked best about the book:

_____

_____

_____

_____

_____

A reason the book resonated at this moment in my life:

_____

_____

_____

_____

_____

How I see the world (or myself) differently having read this book?

_____

_____

_____

_____

_____

Quotes I loved from the book:

_____

_____

_____

_____

_____

_____

_____

_____

_____

_____

_____

_____

_____

_____

BOOKS I'VE FINISHED

Title: _____

When and where I read the book: _____

The kind of book (novel, memoir, poetry, graphic novel, etc.): _____

_____

The plot in one sentence: _____

_____

What I liked best about the book:

_____

_____

_____

_____

_____

A reason the book resonated at this moment in my life:

_____

_____

_____

_____

_____

How I see the world (or myself) differently having read this book?

_____

_____

_____

_____

_____

Quotes I loved from the book:

_____

_____

_____

_____

_____

_____

_____

_____

_____

_____

_____

_____

_____

_____

BOOKS I'VE FINISHED

Title: _____

When and where I read the book: _____

The kind of book (novel, memoir, poetry, graphic novel, etc.): _____
_____

The plot in one sentence: _____
_____

What I liked best about the book:
_____
_____
_____
_____
_____

A reason the book resonated at this moment in my life:
_____
_____
_____
_____
_____

How I see the world (or myself) differently having read this book?

_____

_____

_____

_____

_____

Quotes I loved from the book:

_____

_____

_____

_____

_____

_____

_____

_____

_____

_____

_____

_____

_____

_____

BOOKS I'VE FINISHED

Title: _____

When and where I read the book: _____

The kind of book (novel, memoir, poetry, graphic novel, etc.): _____
_____

The plot in one sentence: _____
_____

What I liked best about the book:
_____
_____
_____
_____
_____

A reason the book resonated at this moment in my life:
_____
_____
_____
_____
_____

How I see the world (or myself) differently having read this book?

_____

_____

_____

_____

_____

Quotes I loved from the book:

_____

_____

_____

_____

_____

_____

_____

_____

_____

_____

_____

_____

_____

_____

_____

BOOKS I'VE FINISHED

Title: _____

When and where I read the book: _____

The kind of book (novel, memoir, poetry, graphic novel, etc.): _____
_____

The plot in one sentence: _____
_____

What I liked best about the book:
_____
_____
_____
_____
_____

A reason the book resonated at this moment in my life:
_____
_____
_____
_____
_____

How I see the world (or myself) differently having read this book?

_____

_____

_____

_____

_____

Quotes I loved from the book:

_____

_____

_____

_____

_____

_____

_____

_____

_____

_____

_____

_____

_____

_____

_____

_____

BOOKS I'VE FINISHED

Title: _____

When and where I read the book: _____

The kind of book (novel, memoir, poetry, graphic novel, etc.): _____
_____

The plot in one sentence: _____
_____

What I liked best about the book:
_____
_____
_____
_____
_____

A reason the book resonated at this moment in my life:
_____
_____
_____
_____
_____

How I see the world (or myself) differently having read this book?

_____

_____

_____

_____

_____

Quotes I loved from the book:

_____

_____

_____

_____

_____

_____

_____

_____

_____

_____

_____

_____

_____

_____

BOOKS I'VE FINISHED

Title: _____

When and where I read the book: _____

The kind of book (novel, memoir, poetry, graphic novel, etc.): _____

_____

The plot in one sentence: _____

_____

What I liked best about the book:

_____

_____

_____

_____

_____

A reason the book resonated at this moment in my life:

_____

_____

_____

_____

_____

How I see the world (or myself) differently having read this book?

_____

_____

_____

_____

_____

Quotes I loved from the book:

_____

_____

_____

_____

_____

_____

_____

_____

_____

_____

_____

_____

_____

_____

_____

BOOKS I'VE FINISHED

Title: _____

When and where I read the book: _____

The kind of book (novel, memoir, poetry, graphic novel, etc.): _____

_____

The plot in one sentence: _____

_____

What I liked best about the book:

_____

_____

_____

_____

_____

A reason the book resonated at this moment in my life:

_____

_____

_____

_____

_____

How I see the world (or myself) differently having read this book?

_____

_____

_____

_____

_____

Quotes I loved from the book:

_____

_____

_____

_____

_____

_____

_____

_____

_____

_____

_____

_____

_____

_____

BOOKS I'VE FINISHED

Title: _____

When and where I read the book: _____

The kind of book (novel, memoir, poetry, graphic novel, etc.): _____
_____

The plot in one sentence: _____
_____

What I liked best about the book:
_____
_____
_____
_____
_____

A reason the book resonated at this moment in my life:
_____
_____
_____
_____
_____

How I see the world (or myself) differently having read this book?

_____

_____

_____

_____

_____

Quotes I loved from the book:

_____

_____

_____

_____

_____

_____

_____

_____

_____

_____

_____

_____

_____

_____

> **She read books as one would breathe air, to fill up and live.**
>
> —ANNIE DILLARD

BOOKS I'VE FINISHED

Title: _____

When and where I read the book: _____

The kind of book (novel, memoir, poetry, graphic novel, etc.): _____

_____

The plot in one sentence: _____

_____

What I liked best about the book:

_____

_____

_____

_____

_____

A reason the book resonated at this moment in my life:

_____

_____

_____

_____

_____

How I see the world (or myself) differently having read this book?

_____

_____

_____

_____

_____

Quotes I loved from the book:

_____

_____

_____

_____

_____

_____

_____

_____

_____

_____

_____

_____

_____

_____

_____

BOOKS I'VE FINISHED

Title: _____

When and where I read the book: _____

The kind of book (novel, memoir, poetry, graphic novel, etc.): _____

_____

The plot in one sentence: _____

_____

What I liked best about the book:

_____

_____

_____

_____

_____

A reason the book resonated at this moment in my life:

_____

_____

_____

_____

_____

How I see the world (or myself) differently having read this book?

_____

_____

_____

_____

_____

Quotes I loved from the book:

_____

_____

_____

_____

_____

_____

_____

_____

_____

_____

_____

_____

_____

_____

BOOKS I'VE FINISHED

Title: _____

When and where I read the book: _____

The kind of book (novel, memoir, poetry, graphic novel, etc.): _____

_____

The plot in one sentence: _____

_____

What I liked best about the book:

_____

_____

_____

_____

_____

A reason the book resonated at this moment in my life:

_____

_____

_____

_____

_____

How I see the world (or myself) differently having read this book?

_____

_____

_____

_____

_____

Quotes I loved from the book:

_____

_____

_____

_____

_____

_____

_____

_____

_____

_____

_____

_____

_____

_____

BOOKS I'VE FINISHED

Title: _____

When and where I read the book: _____

The kind of book (novel, memoir, poetry, graphic novel, etc.): _____

_____

The plot in one sentence: _____

_____

What I liked best about the book:

_____

_____

_____

_____

_____

A reason the book resonated at this moment in my life:

_____

_____

_____

_____

_____

How I see the world (or myself) differently having read this book?

_____

_____

_____

_____

_____

Quotes I loved from the book:

_____

_____

_____

_____

_____

_____

_____

_____

_____

_____

_____

_____

_____

_____

_____

BOOKS I'VE FINISHED

Title: _____

When and where I read the book: _____

The kind of book (novel, memoir, poetry, graphic novel, etc.): _____
_____

The plot in one sentence: _____
_____

What I liked best about the book:
_____
_____
_____
_____
_____

A reason the book resonated at this moment in my life:
_____
_____
_____
_____
_____

How I see the world (or myself) differently having read this book?

_____

_____

_____

_____

_____

Quotes I loved from the book:

_____

_____

_____

_____

_____

_____

_____

_____

_____

_____

_____

_____

_____

_____

_____

_____

BOOKS I'VE FINISHED

Title: _____

When and where I read the book: _____

The kind of book (novel, memoir, poetry, graphic novel, etc.): _____

_____

The plot in one sentence: _____

_____

What I liked best about the book:

_____

_____

_____

_____

_____

A reason the book resonated at this moment in my life:

_____

_____

_____

_____

_____

How I see the world (or myself) differently having read this book?

_____

_____

_____

_____

_____

Quotes I loved from the book:

_____

_____

_____

_____

_____

_____

_____

_____

_____

_____

_____

_____

_____

_____

BOOKS I'VE FINISHED

Title: _____

When and where I read the book: _____

The kind of book (novel, memoir, poetry, graphic novel, etc.): _____

_____

The plot in one sentence: _____

_____

What I liked best about the book:

_____

_____

_____

_____

_____

A reason the book resonated at this moment in my life:

_____

_____

_____

_____

_____

How I see the world (or myself) differently having read this book?

_____

_____

_____

_____

_____

Quotes I loved from the book:

_____

_____

_____

_____

_____

_____

_____

_____

_____

_____

_____

_____

_____

_____

_____

_____

BOOKS I'VE FINISHED

Title: _____

When and where I read the book: _____

The kind of book (novel, memoir, poetry, graphic novel, etc.): _____

_____

The plot in one sentence: _____

_____

What I liked best about the book:

_____

_____

_____

_____

_____

A reason the book resonated at this moment in my life:

_____

_____

_____

_____

_____

How I see the world (or myself) differently having read this book?

_____

_____

_____

_____

_____

Quotes I loved from the book:

_____

_____

_____

_____

_____

_____

_____

_____

_____

_____

_____

_____

_____

_____

BOOKS I'VE FINISHED

Title: _____

When and where I read the book: _____

The kind of book (novel, memoir, poetry, graphic novel, etc.): _____

_____

The plot in one sentence: _____

_____

What I liked best about the book:

_____

_____

_____

_____

_____

A reason the book resonated at this moment in my life:

_____

_____

_____

_____

_____

How I see the world (or myself) differently having read this book?

_____

_____

_____

_____

_____

Quotes I loved from the book:

_____

_____

_____

_____

_____

_____

_____

_____

_____

_____

_____

_____

_____

_____

BOOKS I'VE FINISHED

Title: _____

When and where I read the book: _____

The kind of book (novel, memoir, poetry, graphic novel, etc.): _____
_____

The plot in one sentence: _____
_____

What I liked best about the book:
_____
_____
_____
_____
_____

A reason the book resonated at this moment in my life:
_____
_____
_____
_____
_____

How I see the world (or myself) differently having read this book?

_____

_____

_____

_____

_____

Quotes I loved from the book:

_____

_____

_____

_____

_____

_____

_____

_____

_____

_____

_____

_____

_____

_____

BOOKS I'VE FINISHED

Title: _____

When and where I read the book: _____

The kind of book (novel, memoir, poetry, graphic novel, etc.): _____

_____

The plot in one sentence: _____

_____

What I liked best about the book:

_____

_____

_____

_____

_____

A reason the book resonated at this moment in my life:

_____

_____

_____

_____

_____

How I see the world (or myself) differently having read this book?

_____

_____

_____

_____

_____

Quotes I loved from the book:

_____

_____

_____

_____

_____

_____

_____

_____

_____

_____

_____

_____

_____

_____

BOOKS I'VE FINISHED

Title: _____

When and where I read the book: _____

The kind of book (novel, memoir, poetry, graphic novel, etc.): _____
_____

The plot in one sentence: _____
_____

What I liked best about the book:

_____
_____
_____
_____
_____

A reason the book resonated at this moment in my life:

_____
_____
_____
_____
_____

How I see the world (or myself) differently having read this book?

_____

_____

_____

_____

_____

Quotes I loved from the book:

_____

_____

_____

_____

_____

_____

_____

_____

_____

_____

_____

_____

_____

_____

_____

BOOKS TO READ NEXT

Use these pages to keep track of recommendations so you won't be left without a book—something a friend recommended, something your book club would never read, something that got a great review, etc.

TITLE	AUTHOR

GENRE	WHY

BOOKS TO READ NEXT

TITLE	AUTHOR

GENRE	WHY

BOOKS TO READ NEXT

TITLE	AUTHOR

BOOKS TO READ NEXT

TITLE	AUTHOR

GENRE	WHY

BOOKS TO READ NEXT

TITLE	AUTHOR

GENRE	WHY

"
I consider reading a good book
a sacred indulgence.

—OPRAH

Oprah's Book Club

Reading one hundred books together? I don't think I ever imagined that, way back in 1996 when the book club launched, but what a wonderful reading journey it's been so far. Maybe you'll find inspiration for your next read among this selection of my OBC picks...

Oprah's Book Club

THE FIRST 102 SELECTIONS FROM OPRAH'S BOOK CLUB

- THE DEEP END OF THE OCEAN
- SONG OF SOLOMON
- THE BOOK OF RUTH
- SHE'S COME UNDONE
- STONES FROM THE RIVER
- THE RAPTURE OF CANAAN
- SONGS IN ORDINARY TIME
- THE HEART OF A WOMAN
- A LESSON BEFORE DYING

- ELLEN FOSTER
- A VIRTUOUS WOMAN
- THE MEANEST THING TO SAY
- THE TREASURE HUNT
- THE BEST WAY TO PLAY
- PARADISE
- HERE ON EARTH
- BLACK AND BLUE
- BREATH, EYES, MEMORY

- I KNOW THIS MUCH IS TRUE
- WHAT LOOKS LIKE CRAZY ON AN ORDINARY DAY
- MIDWIVES
- WHERE THE HEART IS
- JEWEL
- THE READER
- THE PILOT'S WIFE
- WHITE OLEANDER
- MOTHER OF PEARL
- TARA ROAD
- RIVER, CROSS MY HEART
- VINEGAR HILL
- A MAP OF THE WORLD
- GAP CREEK
- DAUGHTER OF FORTUNE
- BACK ROADS
- THE BLUEST EYE
- WHILE I WAS GONE
- THE POISONWOOD BIBLE
- OPEN HOUSE
- DROWNING RUTH
- HOUSE OF SAND AND FOG

- WE WERE THE MULVANEYS
- ICY SPARKS
- STOLEN LIVES
- CANE RIVER
- THE CORRECTIONS
- A FINE BALANCE
- FALL ON YOUR KNEES
- SULA
- EAST OF EDEN
- CRY, THE BELOVED COUNTRY
- ONE HUNDRED YEARS OF SOLITUDE
- THE HEART IS A LONELY HUNTER
- ANNA KARENINA
- THE GOOD EARTH
- AS I LAY DYING
- THE SOUND AND THE FURY
- LIGHT IN AUGUST
- A MILLION LITTLE PIECES
- NIGHT
- THE MEASURE OF A MAN
- THE ROAD
- MIDDLESEX

- LOVE IN THE TIME OF CHOLERA
- THE PILLARS OF THE EARTH
- A NEW EARTH
- THE STORY OF EDGAR SAWTELLE
- SAY YOU'RE ONE OF THEM
- FREEDOM
- GREAT EXPECTATIONS
- A TALE OF TWO CITIES
- WILD
- THE TWELVE TRIBES OF HATTIE
- THE INVENTION OF WINGS
- RUBY
- THE UNDERGROUND RAILROAD
- LOVE WARRIOR
- BEHOLD THE DREAMERS
- AN AMERICAN MARRIAGE
- THE SUN DOES SHINE
- BECOMING
- THE WATER DANCER
- OLIVE, AGAIN

- AMERICAN DIRT
- HIDDEN VALLEY ROAD
- DEACON KING KONG
- CASTE
- JACK
- LILA
- HOME
- GILEAD
- THE SWEETNESS OF WATER
- THE LOVE SONGS OF W.E.B. DU BOIS
- BEWILDERMENT
- THE WAY OF INTEGRITY
- FINDING ME
- NIGHTCRAWLING
- THAT BIRD HAS MY WINGS
- DEMON COPPERHEAD
- BITTERSWEET
- HELLO BEAUTIFUL
- THE COVENANT OF WATER
- WELLNESS

Oprah's Book Club

FUN FACTS

NUMBER OF BOOKS, 1996 TO 2023:

102

BESTSELLING PICK OF ALL TIME:

A Tale of Two Cities

BY CHARLES DICKENS

(200 million, minus a few undocumented 19th century sales)

TOTAL NUMBER OF PAGES READ:

39,630

(give or take a foreign edition)

BOOKS MADE INTO MOVIES:

34

OPRAH EDITION COPIES SOLD IN THE FIRST 15 YEARS OF THE BOOK CLUB:

OVER 55 MILLION

BOOKS THAT TAKE PLACE IN CALIFORNIA, NEW YORK, OR WISCONSIN:

19

BOOKS IN WHICH WOMEN—WHO AREN'T NUNS!—TAKE UP RESIDENCE IN A CONVENT: 2

BOOKS MADE INTO AN HBO MINISERIES:

1

BOOKS WRITTEN BY A DEBUT AUTHOR: 24

BOOKS WRITTEN AFTER THE AUTHOR'S 60TH BIRTHDAY:

15

AVERAGE NUMBER OF BOOKS AN AUTHOR PUBLISHED BEFORE THEIR BOOK CLUB SELECTION:

3.7

BOOKS ORIGINALLY WRITTEN IN ANOTHER LANGUAGE:

7

BOOKS TRANSLATED BY THE AUTHOR'S SPOUSE:

1

Night

BY ELIE WIESEL

"

I think the best books unlatch something within.

—IMANI PERRY

"

Life-transforming ideas have always come to me through books.

—BELL HOOKS

MEMOIRS:

10

AUTHORS WHO HAVE WON AN OSCAR:

2

AUTHORS WHO HAVE RECEIVED HONORARY KNIGHTHOODS FROM THE QUEEN OF ENGLAND:

2

AUTHORS PICKED MORE THAN ONCE:

11

AUTHORS WHO HAD THEIR WORK PRESERVED IN THE NATIONAL MILLENNIUM TIME CAPSULE (TO BE OPENED IN 2100): **4**

NATIONAL BOOK AWARDS–WINNING AUTHORS:

9

THE BOOK THAT MADE OPRAH SAY: "WHEN I READ IT, IT FELT LIKE COMING HOME":

The Love Songs of W.E.B. Du Bois,
BY HONORÉE FANONNE JEFFERS

BOOKS THAT ARE 400 OR MORE PAGES:

37

BOOKS THAT MADE GAYLE SAY, "OPRAH, JUST TELL ME WHAT'S GOING TO HAPPEN NEXT—I'M AFRAID TO TURN THE PAGE":

1

The Water Dancer
BY TA-NEHISI COATES

BOOKS THAT OPRAH CONSIDERS "REQUIRED READING FOR ALL HUMANITY":

2

Night
BY ELIE WIESEL
AND
Caste
BY ISABEL WILKERSON

NOVELS:

84

Oprah's
Book Club

OPRAH'S FAVORITE FIRST SENTENCES

Some opening sentences stick with you forever...

"There's no way to know the exact second your life changes forever."
THE SUN DOES SHINE: HOW I FOUND LIFE AND FREEDOM ON DEATH ROW, BY ANTHONY RAY HINTON

"They shoot the white girl first. With the rest they can take their time."
PARADISE, BY TONI MORRISON

"All happy families are alike; each unhappy family is unhappy in its own way."
ANNA KARENINA, BY LEO TOLSTOY

"I spent much of my childhood listening to the sound of striving."
BECOMING, BY MICHELLE OBAMA

"Ruby Bell was a constant reminder of what could befall a woman whose standards were too high."
RUBY, BY CYNTHIA BOND

"On the morning of her ninth birthday, the day after Madame Françoise Derbanne slapped her, Suzette peed on the rosebushes."
CANE RIVER, BY LALITA TADEMY

"First, I got myself born."
DEMON COPPERHEAD, BY BARBARA KINGSOLVER

"There was a time in Africa the people could fly."
THE INVENTION OF WINGS, BY SUE MONK KIDD

"It was the best of times, it was the worst of times, it was the age of wisdom, it was the age of foolishness, it was the epoch of belief, it was the epoch of incredulity, it was the season of Light, it was the season of Darkness, it was the spring of hope..."
A TALE OF TWO CITIES, BY CHARLES DICKENS

"There are two kinds of people in the world, those who leave home, and those who don't."
AN AMERICAN MARRIAGE, BY TAYARI JONES

> 66

**Stories have given me a place
in which to lose myself.**

—ROXANE GAY

AT THIS POINT, my hope is this journal has helped you track your reading journey: the books that once took you to far-flung worlds, struck close to home, or sparked aha moments. Books that practically demanded to be shared with friends and family. Books that maybe even reconnected you with what it means to be human. You have gathered the quotes you wish to remember— and the writers you never want to forget.

Not to mention lists with your next great read...and the one after that...and after that, too. From one reader to another, I wish you so many more blissful hours with a book at hand.

Oprah

FOUNDER AND EDITORIAL DIRECTOR, OPRAH DAILY: **Oprah Winfrey**
EDITOR AT LARGE, OPRAH DAILY: **Gayle King**
EDITORIAL DIRECTOR, OPRAH DAILY: **Pilar Guzmán**
CREATIVE DIRECTOR, OPRAH DAILY: **Adam Glassman**
CONTRIBUTING EDITOR AND WRITER: **M. D. Healey**
DIRECTOR OF PHOTOGRAPHY: **Christina Weber**
BOOKS DIRECTOR, PRINT AND DIGITAL, OPRAH DAILY: **Leigh Newman**

CREATIVE DIRECTOR, HEARST PRODUCT STUDIO: **Gillian MacLeod**
SR. MANAGER, HEARST PRODUCT STUDIO: **Missy Steinberg Bisaccia**

PHOTOGRAPHY: Oprah Daily/Ruven Afanador: 4, 204, 207;
O, The Oprah Magazine/Ruven Afanador: 2;
Adobe Stock: AC Photography: 44; ArgitopIA: 8;
BlueOrange Studio: 158; debramillet: 199; hiddencatch: 200;
joda: 132; Olha Rohulya: 106; Sebastien Coell: 72;
simon: half-jacket; stefanotermanini: 26;
The Camera Queen: 194; topntp: 202

Library of Congress Cataloging-in-Publication Data
is on file with the publisher.

ISBN 978-1-956300-04-8

Printed in China

2 4 6 8 10 9 7 5 3 1 hardcover

H E A R S T

It's Your Time to Thrive!

Discover essential tools from Oprah Daily, including inspiring products and an all-access Oprah Insider membership, designed to help you manifest your goals and live your best life.

Oprah Daily

GET MORE OPRAH DAILY AT HOME!
OPRAHDAILY.COM/THRIVE